I0822051

This prayer book belongs to

Holy Spirit Prayer Book

Holy Spirit Prayer Book

Written and compiled by
Mary Mark Wickenhiser, FSP

Pauline
BOOKS & MEDIA
BOSTON

Nihil Obstat:

Reverend Thomas W. Buckley, S.T.D., S.S.L.

Imprimatur:

✠ Seán Cardinal O'Malley, O.F.M. Cap.
Archbishop of Boston
February 19, 2016

ISBN 10: 0-8198-3449-1

ISBN 13: 978-0-8198-3449-2

Cover design by Rosana Usselmann

Published by Pauline Books & Media, 50 Saint Paul's Avenue, Boston, MA 02130-3491

Printed in China.

www.pauline.org

Pauline Books & Media is the publishing house of the Daughters of St. Paul, an international congregation of women religious serving the Church with the communications media.

4 5 6 7 8 9 10 29 28 27 26 25

Contents

Acknowledgments

New Testament Scripture quotations contained herein are from the *The New Testament: St. Paul Catholic Edition,* translated by Mark A. Wauck, copyright © 2000 by the Society of St. Paul, Staten Island, New York, and are used by permission. All rights reserved.

Old Testament Scripture quotations contained herein are from the *New Revised Standard Version Bible: Catholic Edition,* copyright © 1989, 1993, Division of Christian Education of the National Council of the Churches of Christ in the United States of America. Used by permission. All rights reserved.

Quotations from the book of Psalms are taken from *The Psalms: A Translation from the Hebrew,*

Half-title page art: Gian Lorenzo Bernini, *Dove of the Holy Spirit* in the stained glass window above the Cathedra Petri in Saint Peter's Basilica (c. 1660). Source https://commons.wikimedia.org/wiki/File:Dove_window_St_Peters_Basilica_(8504106313).jpg

Introduction

The Holy Spirit is truly God, a distinct person of the Holy Trinity, co-equal and co-eternal with the Father and the Son, sent to us by our heavenly Father and by Jesus Christ to guide, enlighten, comfort, and strengthen us throughout our life's journey. As Catholics we believe that God dwells with us and within us through the gift of the Holy Spirit.

In the New Testament, we are first introduced to the power of the Holy Spirit at the Annunciation (Mt 1:18–24; Lk 1:35). Then, in the Gospel of Luke, as we read about the public ministry of Jesus, we begin to get a better understanding of how the mission of the Holy Spirit is linked to the redemptive mission of Jesus Christ (Lk 3:21–22; 4:14; 4:18; 10:21; 12:12).

In the Gospel of John, especially, Jesus teaches that after his death, when he has returned to his Father, the Spirit will come. The Paraclete or Advocate will pour out his spirit on the Apostles. The work of the Holy Spirit will be to confirm the Apostles in the truth of the Gospel.

John's gospel account of Christ's words speaks clearly of the Holy Spirit as a Person distinct from the Father and the Son: "I will ask the Father and he will give you another Intercessor to be with you forever, the Spirit of Truth . . ." (Jn 14:16).

"When the Intercessor comes, whom I will send to you from the Father—the Spirit of truth who comes forth from the Father—he will bear witness to me . . ." (Jn 15:26). Here we receive a glimpse into the Trinitarian relationship.

The Spirit is distinct from Jesus and there is an essential and intimate relationship among the Father, the Son, and the Spirit. He is their spirit, theirs to send. Jesus told us that when his mission on earth was finished, he would return to his Heavenly Father and they would send the Holy Spirit to continue the work of salvation. Jesus

Christ continues his redemptive work through the presence of the Holy Spirit whose mission it is to fill us with grace and God's presence so that we are able to become adopted children of the Father.

On Pentecost, the Holy Spirit was sent from the Father and the Son with power, just as Jesus had promised (see Acts 2). Timid, insecure, and fearful men were transformed into courageous, confident, and self-sacrificing Apostles on fire with the teachings of Jesus. We speak of the day of Pentecost as the birth of the Church because it was on that day that the promise of Jesus was fulfilled and the Holy Spirit came down on the Apostles to remain with them and with the Church forever. On that day the Church was publicly revealed; the Gospel began to spread to all nations. Initially, the Apostles and disciples of Jesus remained in their own country, but gradually went out to various parts of the world preaching, healing, and baptizing. Saints Peter and Paul eventually made their way to Rome where Peter became the first Bishop of Rome.

The mission of the Church is the same as that of the Spirit: to sanctify—to pour out the graces and merits of Christ's redemption on all men and women, giving us a participation in the life of God. The Holy Spirit is the breath of life, the life-giving principle of every saving action. The Church lives the life of the Spirit, and in the grace of the Holy Spirit, the Church is able to continue the saving work of Christ—proclaiming the gospel; forgiving sins; as well as offering healing to the broken and redemption to those seeking salvation.

Through the Church's ministry, Baptism is imparted by water and the Holy Spirit. Through Confirmation, one is strengthened in virtue by the power of the Holy Spirit. The words of absolution in the sacrament of Penance point to the role of the Holy Spirit in the forgiveness of sins. The words of the sacrament of the Anointing of the Sick invoke the grace of the Holy Spirit. All the gifts that assist us in our pursuit of holiness and growth in grace come from the Holy Spirit, the Sanctifier.

The power of the Holy Spirit is poured into the heart of every believer with the sacraments of Baptism and Confirmation. The Spirit gives us a new life, the life of God within us. When this new life is nurtured and encouraged to grow, it will flourish and increase so that we may become the presence of God to others.

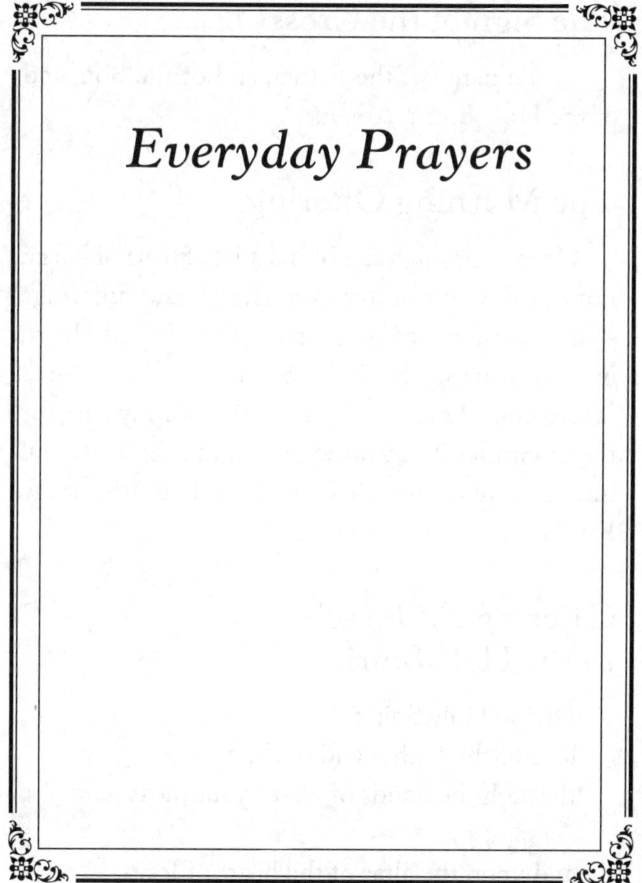

Everyday Prayers

The Sign of the Cross

In the name of the Father, and of the Son, and of the Holy Spirit. Amen.

The Morning Offering

O Jesus, through the Immaculate Heart of Mary, I offer you all my prayers, works, joys, and sufferings of this day, for the intentions of your Sacred Heart, in union with the holy Sacrifice of the Mass throughout the world, in reparation for my sins, for the intentions of my loved ones, and for the general intention recommended this month by the Holy Father.

Offering of Oneself to the Holy Spirit

Divine Holy Spirit,
love of the Father and of the Son,
through the hands of Mary, your most pure
 spouse
and upon the altar of the heart of Jesus,
I offer you myself today

and every day of my life.
I offer you my daily labors,
my every action, my every breath,
with all my love and every beat of my heart.
Grant that today and every day I may heed
your inspiration and, in all things,
accomplish your will. Amen.

Adoration and Praise

I adore you, my God, and I love you with all my heart. I thank you for having created me, made me a Christian, and sustained me through the night. I offer you my actions of this day; grant that they all may be according to your will and for your greater glory. Preserve me from sin and all evil today. May your grace be always with me and with all whom I love. Amen.

The Angelus

℣. The angel spoke God's message to Mary,
℟. and she conceived of the Holy Spirit.

Hail Mary . . .

℣. "I am the lowly servant of the Lord:
℟. "Let it be done to me according to your word."

Hail Mary . . .

℣. And the Word became flesh
℟. and lived among us.

Hail Mary . . .

℣. Pray for us, holy Mother of God,
℟. that we may become worthy of the promises of Christ.

Let us pray.

Lord,
fill our hearts with your grace;
once, through the message of an angel
you revealed to us the incarnation of your Son;
now through his suffering and death
lead us to the glory of his resurrection.
We ask this through Christ our Lord.
Amen.

The Regina Caeli

(Prayed during the Easter Season instead of the Angelus.)

Queen of heaven rejoice, alleluia.
For Christ, your Son and Son of God,
has risen as he said, alleluia.
Pray to God for us, alleluia.

℣. Rejoice and be glad, O Virgin Mary, alleluia.
℟. For the Lord has truly risen, alleluia.

Let us pray.

God of life,
you have given joy to the world
by the resurrection of your Son, our Lord
Jesus Christ.
Through the prayers of his mother, the Virgin
Mary,
bring us to the happiness of eternal life.
We ask this through Christ our Lord.

℟. Amen.

The Lord's Prayer

Our Father, who art in heaven, hallowed be thy name; thy kingdom come; thy will be done on earth as it is in heaven. Give us this day our daily bread, and forgive us our trespasses, as we forgive those who trespass against us, and lead us not into temptation, but deliver us from evil. Amen.

Hail Mary

Hail Mary, full of grace, the Lord is with you. Blessed are you among women, and blessed is the fruit of your womb, Jesus. Holy Mary, Mother of God, pray for us sinners, now and at the hour of our death. Amen.

Glory

Glory to the Father, and to the Son, and to the
Holy Spirit,
as it was in the beginning, is now, and will be
forever. Amen.

An Act of Faith

O my God, I firmly believe that you are one God in three divine Persons: Father, Son, and Holy Spirit; I believe that your divine Son became man and died for our sins, and that he will come to judge the living and the dead. I believe these and all the truths which the holy Catholic Church teaches, because you have revealed them, who can neither deceive nor be deceived.

An Act of Hope

O my God, relying on your infinite goodness and promises, I hope to obtain pardon of my sins, the help of your grace, and life everlasting, through the merits of Jesus Christ, my Lord and Redeemer.

An Act of Love

O my God, I love you above all things, with my whole heart and soul, because you are all-good and worthy of all love. I love my neighbor as myself for the love of you. I forgive all who have injured me, and I ask pardon of all whom I have injured.

An Act of Contrition

O my God, I am heartily sorry for having offended you, and I detest all my sins because of your just punishments, but most of all because they offend you, my God, who are all-good and deserving of all my love. I firmly resolve, with the help of your grace, to sin no more and to avoid the near occasions of sin.

Prayer of Entrustment

Dear and loving Mother Mary, keep your hand upon me this day; guard my mind, my heart, and my senses, that I may not commit sin.

Make my thoughts, affections, words, and actions holy, so that I may be pleasing to you and to your divine Son, Jesus, and attain heaven with you.

Jesus and Mary, give me your holy blessing.

In the name of the Father, and of the Son, and of the Holy Spirit. Amen.

Hail, Holy Queen

Hail, holy Queen, Mother of mercy, our life, our sweetness, and our hope! To you we cry, poor banished children of Eve; to you we send up our sighs, mourning and weeping in this valley of tears. Turn then, most gracious advocate, your eyes of mercy toward us, and after this our exile, show unto us the blessed fruit of your womb, Jesus. O clement, O loving, O sweet Virgin Mary.

To the Guardian Angel

Angel of God, my guardian dear, to whom God's love entrusts me here, ever this day/night be at my side, to light and guard, to rule and guide. Amen.

For the Faithful Departed

Eternal rest grant to them, Lord,
and let perpetual light shine upon them.
May they rest in peace. Amen.

Invocations for a Holy Death

Jesus, Mary, and Joseph, I give you my heart and my soul.
Jesus, Mary, and Joseph, assist me in the hour of my death.
Jesus, Mary, and Joseph, let me die in peace with you.

Morning Prayers

Morning prayer can be a time to give praise and thanks to God, to remind ourselves that God is the source of all good things. Lifting our hearts and minds to God in the early hours of the day can help us put our life into perspective: God is our loving Creator who has our best interest at heart.

I will bless the Lord at all times.
His praise will be ever on my lips.
Glory to the Father, and to the Son, and to the
    Holy Spirit,
as it was in the beginning, is now, and will be
    forever. Amen.

Psalm 57

O God, your loving kindness endures forever.

Be gracious to me, O God, be gracious to me
for my soul takes refuge in you;
indeed, I take refuge in the shelter of your
wings
until the storms of destruction have
passed. . . .
My heart is steadfast, O God, my heart is
steadfast.
I will sing hymns and psalms
Awake, my soul,
awake, lyre and harp,
that I may awake the dawn.
LORD, I will praise you among the peoples,
sing psalms to you among the nations,
for your loving kindness is so great that it
reaches to the heavens,
and your faithfulness to the skies.
O God, be exalted above the heavens,
let your glory be above all the earth.

Glory to the Father . . .

Psalm 104

Glory and praise to you, O Lord, forever.

Bless the Lord, my soul.
Lord, my God, how great you are.
You are robed in splendor and majesty,
clothed in light as a cloak.
You spread out the heavens like a tent,
set the timbers for your lodgings on the waters,
make the clouds your chariot,
and you ride on the wings of the wind.
You establish the winds as messengers,
flames of fire as your ministers.
You fixed the foundations of the earth
so that it shall not be moved for an eternity
of eternities. . . .
I will sing of the Lord as long as I live,
sing psalms to my God while I still have life.
May this meditation of mine be pleasing to
him,
for I rejoice in the Lord.
Bless the Lord, my soul. Alleluia.

Glory to the Father . . .

Psalm 111

Great are your works, O Lord.

Alleluia
I will give thanks to the Lord with all my heart
at the meeting of the upright and in the congregation.
Great are the works of the Lord,
pondered by all who delight in them.
All his work is full of splendor and majesty;
his righteousness endures forever.
He has made a memorial of his wonderful works.
The Lord is gracious and compassionate.
He provides food for those who fear him;
mindful of his covenant forever. . . .
His name is holy and awe-inspiring.
Fear of the Lord is the beginning of wisdom;
those who practice it have good understanding.
His praise endures forever.

Glory to the Father . . .

The Word of God

The Holy Spirit, present in our soul, leads us, enlightens us, and prays in us.

The Spirit also helps us in our weakness, for we do not know how to pray as we should; instead, the Spirit pleads for us with inexpressible groanings, and the One Who is able to see what is in the heart knows what the Spirit wishes, because the Spirit intercedes for all the saints in accordance with God's will. Now we know that God works in every way for the good with those who love God and are called in accordance with his plan (Rm 8:26–28).

Come, Holy Spirit, reveal to me the truth
about God.

(For alternate readings, see page 94 from the Ponder and Pray section.)

From prayer, we draw the strength needed to meet the challenges of daily life as committed followers of Jesus Christ, and, as such, to be living signs of the Lord's loving presence in the world.

Intercessions

Giver of all grace, we thank and praise you for the gift of a new day. With confidence we turn to you and pray:

Response: Lord, send us your Spirit.

Enliven our hearts with the Spirit's gifts of courage, love, and self-control. ℟.

Direct our minds and hearts to the working of your Holy Spirit in our lives. ℟.

Strengthen our faith and encourage us in times of trial and hardship. ℟.

Help us to recognize your presence in one another and those around us. ℟.

Bless our efforts as we strive for mutual understanding, respect, and love within our family. ℟.

Sustain and nourish us in our life commitments and vocations. ℟.

Preserve our young people from the lure of drugs, alcohol, gangs, and violence. ℟.

Help us to act with kindness toward the stranger, the lonely, and the grieving. ℟.

Welcome all the faithful departed into the light of your presence. ℟.

Add any particular intentions you wish, and conclude by praying to our heavenly Father in the words Jesus taught us:

Our Father, who art in heaven . . .

Closing Prayer

Lord, pour into our hearts the Holy Spirit that we may proclaim the praises of your love and seek to serve you alone. Grant this through your Son, Jesus Christ, who lives and reigns with you in the unity of the Holy Spirit, one God, for ever and ever. Amen.

Let us praise the Lord.
And give him thanks.

Evening Prayers

As the day draws to a close, we place ourselves in an attitude of thanksgiving. We take time to express our gratitude to a loving God for his abiding presence. We thank him for the gift of the day and all it has brought with it. We are grateful to God for all the things we were able to achieve throughout the day, and we entrust him with the concerns of tomorrow.

From the rising to the setting of the sun,
may the name of the Lord be praised.
Glory to the Father, and to the Son, and to the
Holy Spirit,
as it was in the beginning, is now, and will be
forever. Amen.

Take a few moments for a brief examination of conscience. Reflect on the ways God acted in your life today, consider how you responded to his invitations to think, speak, and act in a more Christ-like manner, and in what ways you would like to be a more faithful disciple tomorrow.

Psalm 51

Create a clean heart in me, O God.

Be gracious to me, O God, according to your
loving kindness.
In the great tenderness of your love,
blot out my transgressions.
Wash me thoroughly from my guilt
and from my sin cleanse me . . .
Create a clean heart in me, O God.
and renew within me an upright spirit.
Do not cast me out from your presence,
and do not withhold your holy spirit from
me.
Restore to me the joy of your salvation,
and let a spirit of willingness sustain me.

Glory to the Father . . .

Psalm 67

May all peoples and nations praise you, O God.

May God be gracious to us and bless us.
May he let his face shine upon us,
that your way may be known on earth;
and your salvation among all nations.
Let the peoples praise you, O God.
Let all the peoples praise you.
Let the nations sing and shout with joy
for you judge the peoples with righteousness,
and guide the nations on the earth.
Let the peoples praise you, O God.
Let all the peoples praise you.
The earth has brought forth its fruit.
May God, our God, bless us.
May God indeed bless us,
and may all the ends of the earth revere him.

Glory to the Father . . .

Psalm 25

May all peoples and nations praise you, O God.

To you, O LORD, I lift up my soul.
In you, my God I trust:
I shall not be disappointed,
my enemies shall not rejoice at my expense.
Indeed, none of those shall be disappointed
who rely on you. . . .
Give me knowledge of your ways, O LORD;
instruct me in your paths.
Make me walk in your truth and teach me.
Because you are my saving God,
it is on you that I have relied at all times.

Glory to the Father . . .

Novena in Preparation for the Feast of Pentecost

The feast of Pentecost, considered the "birthday" of the Church, commemorates the Holy Spirit's descent upon the Apostles. This novena, in preparation for the feast of Pentecost, commemorates the nine days between the Ascension of Our Lord and the Descent of the Holy Spirit upon the Apostles and Our Lady as they were gathered in the Upper Room praying for the coming of the Paraclete (see Ac 2:1–4).

The novena begins on the Friday after Ascension Thursday, and concludes on Saturday, the vigil of Pentecost. In some dioceses the feast of the Ascension is celebrated on the following Sunday; however, the novena begins on Friday, as noted. It can be prayed in preparation for the feast of Pentecost (or any time you feel the need) during your own prayer time, together with your prayer group, or as a parish community event. The intention in praying the novena is to open ourselves to the work of the Holy Spirit in our lives and to become more deeply aware of the Holy Spirit's power to help us transform our lives and fill us with God's grace and blessings.

The following novena is based on the writings of Blessed James Alberione.

First Day

The Holy Spirit Intercedes for Us

The Holy Spirit is the Spirit of Light, of Strength, and of Love. Through the gifts of the Holy Spirit, the mind is enlightened, the will strengthened, and the heart inflamed with love of God.

> The Spirit also helps us in our weakness, for we do not know how to pray as we should; instead, the Spirit pleads for us . . . and the One Who is able to see what is in the heart knows what the Spirit wishes, because the Spirit intercedes . . . in accordance with God's will.
>
> Romans 8:26–27

Prayer

Almighty and eternal God, renew us by water and the Holy Spirit. Send your sevenfold Spirit and rekindle in us the gifts of wisdom and understanding, counsel and fortitude, knowledge, piety and holy fear of the Lord. Amen

Our Father . . . Hail Mary . . . Glory be . . .

Invocation

Come, Holy Spirit, fill the hearts of your faithful, enkindle in us the fire of your love, and renew the face of the earth.

SECOND DAY

The Gift of Wisdom

The Spirit's gift of wisdom strengthens our faith, fortifies hope, perfects charity, and promotes the practice of virtue in one's life. It enlightens the mind so that we can better appreciate divine things, put God first in our lives, and judge what will be helpful and what can be an obstacle to reaching heaven.

Wisdom gives life to the one who possesses it.

ECCLESIASTES 7:12

Prayer

Come, Spirit of Wisdom, make known to me the power and beauty of heavenly things. Teach me to love them above all the passing joys and satisfactions of this earth. Grant that I may always put the things of God first in my life until that day when I am united with you forever in heaven. Amen.

Our Father . . . Hail Mary . . . Glory be . . .

Invocation

Come, Holy Spirit, fill the hearts of your faithful with the gift of wisdom; enkindle in us the fire of your love that we may proclaim the kingdom of God in word and deed.

Third Day

The Gift of Understanding

The Spirit's gift of understanding helps us to grasp the meaning of the truths of our faith. Through faith we believe; through the gift of understanding we learn to value and appreciate the faith we profess. Understanding helps us to better grasp the inner meaning of revealed truths so that what we believe bears witness in our life.

> "But the [seed] sown on good earth, this is the one who hears the word and understands, who, indeed, bears fruit, and produces a hundredfold, or sixtyfold, or thirtyfold."
>
> Matthew 13:23

Prayer

Come, Spirit of Understanding, enlighten my mind that I may see more deeply into the truths I already believe by faith. Grant that I may one day come to see your eternal light; and in the radiance of glory have a clear vision of you and the Father and the Son. Amen.

Our Father . . . Hail Mary . . . Glory be . . .

Invocation

Come, Holy Spirit, fill the hearts of your faithful with the gift of understanding; enkindle in us the fire of your love that we may proclaim the kingdom of God in word and deed.

FOURTH DAY

The Gift of Counsel

The Spirit's gift of counsel or right judgment enables us to choose the right course of action, especially in difficult circumstances. Counsel helps us direct the principles provided by the gifts of knowledge and understanding to actual situations that confront us in the course of our daily lives. This gift can be considered as supernatural common sense, an invaluable resource in our pursuit of Christian living.

> You [LORD] guide me according to your plan,
> And, in the end, you will take me into splendor.
>
> PSALM 73:24

Prayer

Come, Spirit of Counsel, help and guide me in all my ways so that I may always choose what is right, even in difficult circumstances. Direct my heart to all that is good and lead me along the path of your commandments to the goal of eternal life. Amen.

Our Father . . . Hail Mary . . . Glory be . . .

Invocation

Come, Holy Spirit, fill the hearts of your faithful with the gift of counsel; enkindle in us the fire of your love that we may proclaim the kingdom of God in word and deed.

Fifth Day

The Gift of Fortitude

The Spirit's gift of fortitude or courage strengthens and supports us so that we can meet the challenges of living as intentional Christians. Fortitude reinforces the will so that in the face of difficulty we act conscientiously and with right intention.

> You will be strengthened with all the power of his glorious might so that your steadfastness and patience will be perfected and you may joyfully give thanks to the Father who made you worthy to share in the portion of the saints in light.
>
> Colossians 1:11

Prayer

Come, Spirit of Fortitude, sustain me in time of trouble; strengthen me in time of weakness; give me courage in time of hardship. Guide me in my efforts to live a holy life until the day that I join the saints in heaven to praise you for all eternity. Amen.

Our Father . . . Hail Mary . . . Glory be . . .

Invocation

Come, Holy Spirit, fill the hearts of your faithful with the gift of fortitude; enkindle in us the fire of your love that we may proclaim the kingdom of God in word and deed.

Sixth Day

The Gift of Knowledge

The Spirit's gift of knowledge enables us to evaluate the things of this earth in relation to God. Knowledge reveals to us the insignificance and emptiness of created things and helps us to see and use them only as means to our ultimate goal of heaven and not as goals in themselves. The gift of knowledge helps us to prioritize our life's values and to put first things first.

> . . . that the God of our Lord Jesus Christ, the glorious Father, may give you a spirit of wisdom and revelation by which you will come to a knowledge of him. May the eyes of your hearts be enlightened so you will come to know what the hope is to which he calls you.
>
> Ephesians 1: 17

Prayer

Come, Spirit of Knowledge, grant that I may always see the things of this earth as a means to serve God and my neighbor. Show me how to glorify God in every circumstance of my life and to cherish the friendship of God beyond all else, in hope of the eternal reward you promise to those who are faithful. Amen.

Our Father . . . Hail Mary . . . Glory be . . .

Invocation

Come, Holy Spirit, fill the hearts of your faithful with the gift of knowledge; enkindle in us the fire of your love that we may proclaim the kingdom of God in word and deed.

Seventh Day

The Gift of Piety

The Spirit's gift of piety helps us to love, reverence, and worship God as our Father, and to respect all people as our brothers and sisters, so that our service to both God and others will not be burdensome.

> So I beg you by God's mercy to offer your whole lives as a living sacrifice which will be holy and pleasing to God—this is your spiritual worship. Do not pattern yourselves after the ways of this world; transform yourselves by the renewal of your minds, so you will be able to discern what God's will is, and what is good, pleasing, and perfect.
>
> Romans 12:1–2

Prayer

Come, Spirit of Piety, enkindle in my heart a love for God and my neighbor. Inspire within me a deep respect for others that leads to real concern, compassion, and care for all those in need. Grant that in serving others I may serve you. Amen.

Our Father . . . Hail Mary . . . Glory be . . .

Invocation

Come, Holy Spirit, fill the hearts of your faithful with the gift of piety; enkindle in us the fire of your love that we may proclaim the kingdom of God in word and deed.

Eighth Day

The Gift of Fear of the Lord

The Spirit's gift of fear of the Lord helps us to respect God and to want to please him in everything. It is not a fear of God, but a fear of offending God which arises from an attitude of reverence and awe.

> Fear of the Lord is the beginning of wisdom;
> those who practice it, have a good understanding.
> His praise will last forever.
>
> Psalm 111:10

Prayer

Come, Spirit of Holy Fear, fill my heart with wonder and admiration of you, Creator of all that is good, true, and beautiful. Grant me an outpouring of your grace that I may see your handiwork in the beauty of creation that surrounds me, and rejoice in the presence of your splendor and majesty. Amen.

Our Father . . . Hail Mary . . . Glory be . . .

Invocation

Come, Holy Spirit, fill the hearts of your faithful with the gift of fear of the Lord; enkindle in us the fire of your love that we may proclaim the kingdom of God in word and deed.

Ninth Day

The Spirit in My Life

The gifts of the Holy Spirit prepare us to respond more readily to divine inspiration and cultivate a more consistent practice of virtue. As we grow in the knowledge and love of God under the guidance of the Holy Spirit, our life as committed Christians becomes more sincere and generous, and the practice of virtue becomes more attractive to us. These acts of virtue, which leave the heart filled with joy and consolation, are known as Fruits of the Holy Spirit. These fruits become a powerful incentive to serve God and our neighbor.

> The Spirit's fruit is love, joy, peace, patience, kindness, goodness, faith, gentleness, self-control. There is no law against these things! . . . If we live in the Spirit, let us also follow the Spirit!
>
> Galasians 5:22–23, 25

Prayer

Come, Divine Spirit, fill my heart with your fruits of love, joy, peace, patience, kindness, goodness, faith, gentleness, and self-control. Direct me along the path to holiness; grant that I may always seek and protect the good of others, and that I may serve your kingdom here on earth. Amen.

Our Father . . . Hail Mary . . . Glory be . . .

Invocation

Come, Holy Spirit, fill the hearts of your faithful, enkindle in us the fire of your love, and renew the face of the earth.

Chaplet of the Holy Spirit

The chaplet is prayed as a means to honor the Holy Spirit, and to ask for a particular grace or virtue for oneself or for another. The chaplet can be prayed with beads to provide a way to follow the flow and repetition of the prayers.

The chaplet consists of seven sets of three beads. Before each set of beads, recite the prayer to the Holy Spirit, then using the beads, pray one Our Father, one Hail Mary and one Glory to the Father. Complete the set with the invocation to the Holy Spirit and move on to the next set.

First

The Gift of Wisdom

Come, Holy Spirit, fill the hearts of your faithful with the gift of wisdom and enkindle in them the fire of your love. Send forth your Spirit, O Lord, and they shall be created, and you will renew the face of the earth.

Our Father . . . Hail Mary . . . Glory be . . .

Invocation

O Holy Spirit, beloved of my soul, come and make your home in my heart.

SECOND

The Gift of Understanding

Come, Holy Spirit, fill the hearts of your faithful with the gift of understanding and enkindle in them the fire of your love. Send forth your Spirit, O Lord, and they shall be created, and you will renew the face of the earth.

Our Father . . . Hail Mary . . . Glory be . . .

Invocation

O Holy Spirit, beloved of my soul, come and make your home in my heart.

THIRD

The Gift of Counsel

Come, Holy Spirit, fill the hearts of your faithful with the gift of counsel and enkindle in them the fire of your love. Send forth your Spirit, O Lord, and they shall be created, and you will renew the face of the earth.

Our Father . . . Hail Mary . . . Glory be . . .

Invocation

O Holy Spirit, beloved of my soul, come and make your home in my heart.

Fourth

The Gift of Fortitude

Come, Holy Spirit, fill the hearts of your faithful with the gift of fortitude and enkindle in them the fire of your love. Send forth your Spirit, O Lord, and they shall be created, and you will renew the face of the earth.

Our Father . . . Hail Mary . . . Glory be . . .

Invocation

O Holy Spirit, beloved of my soul, come and make your home in my heart.

Fifth

The Gift of Knowledge

Come, Holy Spirit, fill the hearts of your faithful with the gift of knowledge and enkindle in them the fire of your love. Send forth your Spirit, O Lord, and they shall be created, and you will renew the face of the earth.

Our Father . . . Hail Mary . . . Glory be . . .

Invocation

O Holy Spirit, beloved of my soul, come and make your home in my heart.

Sixth

The Gift of Piety

Come, Holy Spirit, fill the hearts of your faithful with the gift of piety and enkindle in them the fire of your love. Send forth your Spirit, O Lord, and they shall be created, and you will renew the face of the earth.

Our Father . . . Hail Mary . . . Glory be . . .

Invocation

O Holy Spirit, beloved of my soul, come and make your home in my heart.

Seventh

The Gift of Fear of the Lord

Come, Holy Spirit, fill the hearts of your faithful with the gift of fear of the Lord and enkindle in them the fire of your love. Send forth your Spirit, O Lord, and they shall be created, and you will renew the face of the earth.

Our Father . . . Hail Mary . . . Glory be . . .

Invocation

O Holy Spirit, beloved of my soul, come and make your home in my heart.

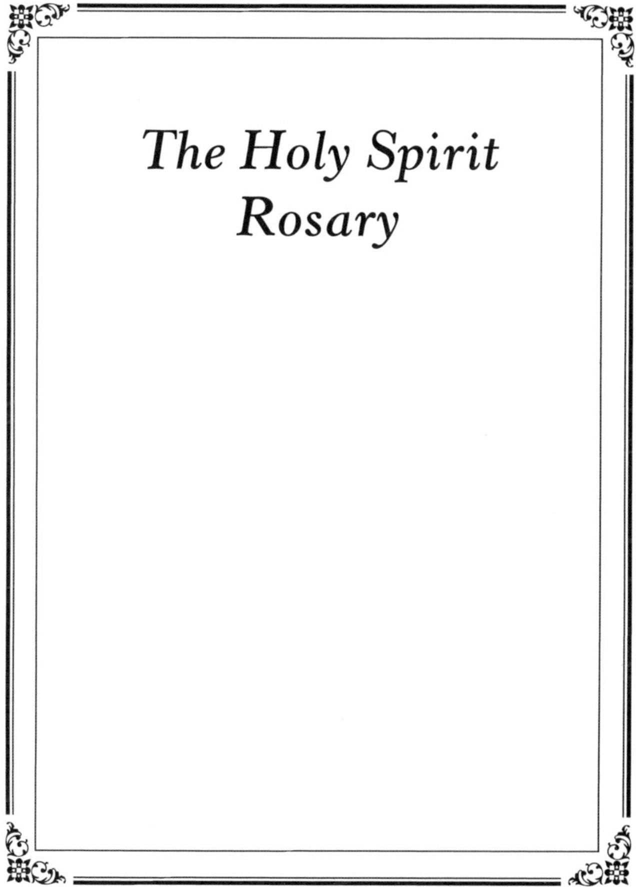

The Holy Spirit Rosary

The Rosary is a blend of contemplative and vocal prayer. When reciting the familiar prayers, we may reflect and meditate on the individual mysteries. Praying the Rosary is a spiritual help to grow in virtue and deepen our prayer life.

The Holy Spirit Rosary is an invitation to pray with our Blessed Mother and contemplate the action of the Holy Spirit in the life of Jesus, in the life of the Church, and in our own lives.

The First Mystery

Jesus is conceived of the Blessed Virgin through the power of the Holy Spirit.

"The Holy Spirit will come upon you.
And the power of the Most High will overshadow
you;
Therefore, the holy child to be born will be called
Son of God." (Lk 1:35)

Grace to ask: For an increase of the theological virtues of faith, hope, and charity.

Our Father, 10 Hail Marys, Glory to the Father . . .

Invocation

Come, Holy Spirit, live in me and conform me to the image of Jesus Christ.

The Second Mystery

The Spirit of the Lord descends upon Jesus at his baptism.

> After he was baptized Jesus at once came up from the water, and, behold, the heavens were opened and he saw the Spirit of God descending upon him like a dove. (Mt 3:16)

Grace to ask: For an increase of the cardinal virtues of prudence, justice, fortitude, and temperance.

Our Father, 10 Hail Marys, Glory to the Father . . .

Invocation

Come, Holy Spirit, lead me by your light, fill me with your grace.

The Third Mystery

Jesus is led by the Holy Spirit into the desert and is tempted by the Devil.

> Jesus returned from the Jordan full of the Holy Spirit and was led by the Spirit through the desert for forty days, while being tempted by the devil. (Lk 4:1)

Grace to ask: For an increase of the gifts of the Holy Spirit—wisdom, understanding, counsel, fortitude, knowledge, piety, and fear of the Lord.

Our Father, 10 Hail Marys, Glory to the Father . . .

Invocation

Come, Holy Spirit, purify my mind, my will, and my heart.

The Fourth Mystery

The Holy Spirit descends upon the Apostles.

Now when the day of Pentecost arrived they were all together in one place. Suddenly a sound like a violent rushing wind came from the sky and filled the house where they were staying. Tongues as of fire appeared to them, parting and coming to rest on each of them, and they were all filled with the Holy Spirit. (Ac 2:1–4)

Grace to ask: for an increase of the fruits of the Holy Spirit—charity, joy, peace, patience, kindness, goodness, generosity, gentleness, faithfulness, modesty, self-control, and chastity.

Our Father, 10 Hail Marys, Glory to the Father . . .

Invocation

Come, Holy Spirit, grant unity to the human family and to the Church, the Body of Christ.

The Fifth Mystery

The Holy Spirit dwells within you.

> Do you not know that you are the temple of God, and that the Spirit of God dwells within you? If anyone destroys God's temple, God will destroy him, for God's temple is holy, and you are that temple. (1 Cor 3:16–17)

Grace to ask: to be renewed and guided by the Holy Spirit.

Our Father, 10 Hail Marys, Glory to the Father . . .

Invocation

Come, Holy Spirit, fill me with yourself and make of me a temple wherein you dwell.

Closing prayer

O God, you instruct the hearts of the faithful by the light of the Holy Spirit. Grant that through the same Holy Spirit we may have a right understanding in all things and ever rejoice in his consolation. Through Christ our Lord. Amen.

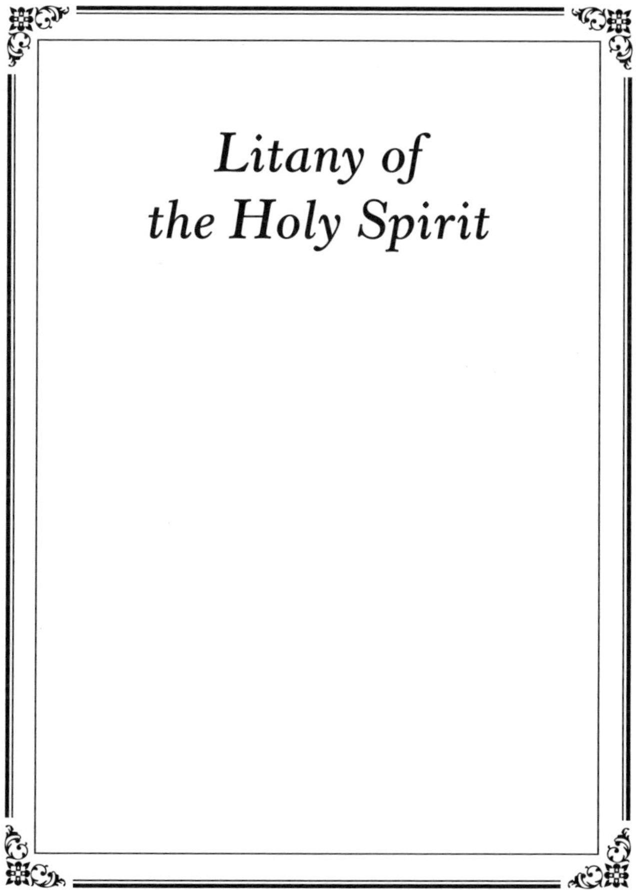

Litany of the Holy Spirit

Lord, *have mercy on us.*

Christ, *have mercy on us.*

Lord, *have mercy on us.*

God, the Father of heaven,
have mercy on us.

God the Son, Redeemer of the world,
save us.

God the Holy Spirit,
sanctify us.

Holy Trinity, one God,
hear us.

Holy Spirit, proceeding from the Father
and the Son,
have mercy on us.

Holy Spirit, co-equal with the Father and the Son,
have mercy on us.

Holy Spirit, Comforter,
have mercy on us.

Holy Spirit, Sanctifier,
have mercy on us.

Holy Spirit, Paraclete,
have mercy on us.

Promise of God the Father,
have mercy on us.

Gift of God Most High,
have mercy on us.

Ray of heavenly light,
have mercy on us.

Author of all good,
have mercy on us.

Source of Living Water,
have mercy on us.

Consuming Fire,
have mercy on us.

Burning love,
have mercy on us.

Spirit who in the beginning moved over the waters,
have mercy on us.

Spirit who overshadowed Mary that she might conceive and give birth to Jesus,
have mercy on us.

Spirit who descended upon Jesus at his baptism,
have mercy on us.

Spirit who on the day of Pentecost rested upon the disciples in the form of tongues of fire,
have mercy on us.

Spirit who at our baptism gives us birth into the divine life,
have mercy on us.

Spirit who dwells in us,
have mercy on us.

Spirit who builds, animates, and sanctifies the Church,
have mercy on us.

Spirit of truth,
have mercy on us.

Spirit of wisdom and understanding,
have mercy on us.

Spirit of right judgment and courage,
have mercy on us.

Spirit of knowledge and of love,
have mercy on us.

Spirit of reverence,
have mercy on us.

Spirit of grace and prayer,
have mercy on us.

Spirit of peace and joy,
have mercy on us.

Spirit of patience and goodness,
have mercy on us.

Spirit of modesty and chastity,
have mercy on us.

Spirit of adoption of the children of God,
have mercy on us.

That you enlighten our minds with holy inspiration, we beseech you,
hear us.

That you inflame our hearts with the fire of your love, we beseech you,
hear us.

That you open to us the treasures of your grace, we beseech you,
hear us.

That you guide us along the path to holiness of life, we beseech you,
hear us.

That you teach us how to pray with humility and trust, we beseech you,
hear us.

That you clothe us with love toward all peoples,
we beseech you,
hear us.

That you fill us with loathing for sin and evil,
we beseech you,
hear us.

That you direct us in the practice of good,
we beseech you,
hear us.

That you grant us the grace to persevere in virtue throughout our life, we beseech you,
hear us.

That at the end of our life here on earth, you will be our everlasting reward, we beseech you,
hear us.

Lamb of God, you take away the sins of the world,
spare us, O Lord.

Lamb of God, you take away the sins of the world,
hear us, O Lord.

Lamb of God, you take away the sins of the world,
have mercy on us.

℣. Come, Holy Spirit, fill the hearts of your faithful.

℟. And kindle in them the fire of your love.

Let us pray.

Merciful Father, grant that your divine Spirit may enlighten, inflame, and cleanse our hearts. May he penetrate us with his heavenly dew and make us fruitful in good works. Through Jesus Christ our Lord. Amen.

Praying with the Holy Spirit in Scripture

The practice of praying with Scripture introduces us to the power of the word of God. Thoughtfully we probe the spiritual meaning of the word to discover the fruits and challenges that Scripture offers to us. Reflective reading allows the Holy Spirit to inspire a deeper understanding of the importance and meaning of the word of God in our lives. When we ponder the words of Scripture, we invite the Spirit to speak more deeply to our hearts. "The word of God is living and active . . . it can discern the innermost thoughts and intentions of the heart" (Heb 4:12).

Before Reading Sacred Scripture

Open my heart, O Holy Spirit, to receive your inspired word. Grant me wisdom to understand what you want to teach me and strength of will to follow wherever you lead.

After Reading Sacred Scripture

I thank you, Holy Spirit, for the word you have spoken to me through the treasure of the Scripture. Make these words a living reality in my life—a constant guide, a lamp for my feet and a light to my path. Amen.

Prayers from Scripture

Come, Holy Spirit, guide us.
Work in us with your gifts
so that your presence may be shown
and we may serve in different ways
for the good of all.

See 1 Corinthians 12:4–8

Spirit of the Living God,
you alone search out everything,
even the depths of God's intentions.
Remain with us always that we may know
all that God has freely bestowed on us,
that we may rightly judge and value all things.

See 1 Corinthians 2:10–15

Lead me, O Holy Spirit,
that I may put to death
all sinful thoughts and actions.
Lead me, O Holy Spirit,
that I may live as God's child.
Lead me, O Holy Spirit,
that I may be free from slavery to sin.
Lead me, O Holy Spirit,
that I may pray and cry out,
"Abba, Father!"
Lead me, O Holy Spirit,
that I may possess the inheritance
of grace that awaits me.

See Romans 8:13–17

Come, Spirit of Truth, and
lead us to the whole truth.
Speak to us of Jesus so that
we may speak of him to others.

See John 16:13–15

Come, Holy Spirit, and help us
in our weakness, for we do not know
how to pray as we should.
Intercede for us so that
the One who sees into our hearts
and knows our thoughts
may hear our prayers.

See Romans 8:26–27

Glorious Father,
give us the Holy Spirit to make us wise
so that we may come to know you.
Enlighten the eyes of our hearts
that we may know the hope
to which you have called us,

the rich blessings you have promised,
and how great is your power
at work in those who believe.

SEE EPHESIANS 1:16–19

Lord God,
fill us with knowledge of your will
through the wisdom and spiritual understanding
your Spirit bestows on your faithful ones
so that we may conduct ourselves in a worthy manner,
be fruitful in every type of work,
and do always what is pleasing to you.

SEE COLOSSIANS 1:9–10

Ponder and Pray with Scripture

A prayerful reading of Scripture opens our hearts to hear God's call more clearly in our daily life. By regular reading and reflection on the words of Scripture, we allow ourselves to be challenged, moved, and enlightened. As our soul is fed and nourished by this word, we can grow in a deeper understanding of the things of God and God's plan for us.

Before reading Scripture, pause for a moment, relax and quiet your mind. Direct your thoughts to the Holy Spirit who dwells within you and who will accompany you as you pray.

Opening Prayer

Come, Holy Spirit, open my heart to receive God's word. Enlighten my mind to understand it and reveal to me the things of God. Strengthen my will to follow your guidance, and help me to bear abundant fruit for the kingdom of God. Amen.

Ponder One of the Following Passages

Because of this I bend my knees to the Father. From him every family in the heavens and on earth is named, so that from the riches of his glory he may grant you inner strength and power through his Spirit. May Christ dwell in your hearts through faith, firmly rooted and established in love, so that with all the saints you may be able to understand the breadth, the length, the height, and the depth, and know Christ's love which surpasses all knowledge so that you may be filled with all God's fullness.

Ephesians 3:14–19

Do you not know that you are the temple of God, and that the Spirit of God dwells within you? If anyone destroys God's temple, God will destroy him, for God's temple is holy, and you are that temple!

Do not deceive yourselves! If any of you think you are wise in this age, become foolish, so you will be *truly* wise. The wisdom of this world is foolishness to God.

1 Corinthians 3:16–19

What eye has not seen nor ear heard,
what human heart has not conceived,
What God has prepared for those who
love him,

this God has revealed to us through his Spirit, for the Spirit is able to search out everything, even the depths of God's intentions. For who can know what someone intends? Surely only that person's own spirit knows! So, too, no one knows what God intends except the Spirit of God. But the Spirit we have received is not the spirit of this world but the Spirit that comes from God and enables us to know what it is that God has freely bestowed upon us. And we proclaim this in words taught by the Spirit rather than by human wisdom, words which explain spiritual matters to those who have the Spirit.

1 Corinthians 2:10–13

Now that we have been restored to his fellowship by faith we are at peace with God through our Lord Jesus Christ. Through him we have obtained access [by faith] to God's grace in which we now stand, and we rejoice in our hope of sharing in God's glory. Not only that, we even rejoice in our afflictions, since we know that affliction produces

co-heirs with Christ, if we suffer with him so as to be glorified with him as well.

ROMANS 8:14–17

Remember

He saved us through the bath of rebirth
and renewal in the Holy Spirit . . .
so that we might be restored to
fellowship with God by his grace
and become heirs in hope of eternal life.

TITUS 3:5–7

Pray

Lord our God, may the Holy Spirit transform our hearts and increase in us the fruits of *charity, joy, peace, patience, kindness, goodness, generosity, gentleness, faithfulness, modesty, self-control,* and *chastity.* May we reach out to others, doing all we can to build up your kingdom here on earth. We ask this through your Son, our Lord Jesus Christ, in the unity of the Holy Spirit, one God forever and ever. Amen.

Glory to the Father . . . (three times)

Day Two

Jesus Does Not Leave Us Orphans

Pray

Lord our God, through the light of your Holy Spirit you instruct the hearts of the faithful, your sons and daughters. Grant that we may always be docile to the Spirit working in our lives, that we may know and appreciate what is right and good and so find happiness in your presence. Help us to recognize the Spirit's invitation to service and respond with joy and eagerness. We ask this through your Son, Jesus Christ our Lord, in the unity of the Holy Spirit, one God forever and ever. Amen.

Read and Ponder

I will not leave you orphaned—
  I will come to you.
In a little while the world will no longer
  see me, but you will see me;
because I will live, you, too, will live.
  On that day you will realize that
I am in my Father,
  and you in me and I in you.

John 14:18–20

I will ask the Father and he will give you
another Intercessor to be with you forever,
the Spirit of truth. . . .
He will remain with you and be in you.

John 14:16–17

Remember

He saved us through the bath of rebirth
and renewal in the Holy Spirit . . .
so that we might be restored to
fellowship with God by his grace
and become heirs in hope of eternal life.

Titus 3:5–7

Pray

Lord our God, may the Holy Spirit transform our hearts and increase in us the fruits of *charity, joy, peace, patience, kindness, goodness, generosity, gentleness, faithfulness, modesty, self-control,* and *chastity*. May we reach out to others, doing all we can to build up your kingdom here on earth. We ask this through your Son, our Lord Jesus Christ, in the unity of the Holy Spirit, one God forever and ever. Amen.

Glory to the Father . . . (three times)

Day Three

We Are Dwelling Places of God

Pray

Lord our God, through the light of your Holy Spirit you instruct the hearts of the faithful, your sons and daughters. Grant that we may always be docile to the Spirit working in our lives, that we may know and appreciate what is right and good and so find happiness in your presence. Help us to recognize the Spirit's invitation to service and respond with joy and eagerness. We ask this through your Son, Jesus Christ our Lord, in the unity of the Holy Spirit, one God forever and ever. Amen.

Read and Ponder

> Do you not know that your bodies are temples of the Holy Spirit within you, who comes to you from God, and that you do not belong to yourselves? You were bought for a price, so glorify God in your bodies!
>
> 1 Corinthians 6:19–20

The Spirit is the life-giver,
the flesh is profitless;
the words I speak to you are
Spirit and life.

John 6:63

Remember

He saved us through the bath of rebirth
and renewal in the Holy Spirit . . .
so that we might be restored to
fellowship with God by his grace
and become heirs in hope of eternal life.

Titus 3:5–7

Pray

Lord our God, may the Holy Spirit transform our hearts and increase in us the fruits of *charity, joy, peace, patience, kindness, goodness, generosity, gentleness, faithfulness, modesty, self-control,* and *chastity*. May we reach out to others, doing all we can to build up your kingdom here on earth. We ask this through your Son, our Lord Jesus Christ, in the unity of the Holy Spirit, one God forever and ever. Amen.

Glory to the Father . . . (three times)

Day Four

We Have the Strength of the Spirit within Us

Pray

Lord our God, through the light of your Holy Spirit you instruct the hearts of the faithful, your sons and daughters. Grant that we may always be docile to the Spirit working in our lives, that we may know and appreciate what is right and good and so find happiness in your presence. Help us to recognize the Spirit's invitation to service and respond with joy and eagerness. We ask this through your Son, Jesus Christ our Lord, in the unity of the Holy Spirit, one God forever and ever. Amen.

Read and Ponder

> I will give them one heart, and put a new spirit within them; I will remove the heart of stone from their flesh and give them a heart of flesh. . . . Then they shall be my people, and I will be their God.
>
> Ezekiel 11:19–20

And this hope is no illusion, because God's love has been poured out in our hearts through the Holy Spirit which has been given to us.

ROMANS 5:5

There are various ways to be active, but the same God who causes all these effects in everyone. . . . One and the same Spirit causes all this, distributing individually to each as he wishes.

1 CORINTHIANS 12:6, 11

Remember

He saved us through the bath of rebirth
and renewal in the Holy Spirit . . .
so that we might be restored to
fellowship with God by his grace
and become heirs in hope of eternal life.

TITUS 3:5–7

Pray

Lord our God, may the Holy Spirit transform our hearts and increase in us the fruits of *charity, joy, peace, patience, kindness, goodness, generosity, gentleness, faithfulness, modesty, self-control,* and *chastity.*

May we reach out to others, doing all we can to build up your kingdom here on earth. We ask this through your Son, our Lord Jesus Christ, in the unity of the Holy Spirit, one God forever and ever. Amen.

Glory to the Father . . . (three times)

Day Five

The Spirit Teaches Us to Pray

Pray

Lord our God, through the light of your Holy Spirit you instruct the hearts of the faithful, your sons and daughters. Grant that we may always be docile to the Spirit working in our lives, that we may know and appreciate what is right and good and so find happiness in your presence. Help us to recognize the Spirit's invitation to service and respond with joy and eagerness. We ask this through your Son, Jesus Christ our Lord, in the unity of the Holy Spirit, one God forever and ever. Amen.

Read and Ponder

Show me the way I should go,
    for to you I lift up my soul.
Rescue me from my enemies, O Lord,
    for I hide myself in you.
Teach me to do your will,
    for you are my God;
may your good Spirit lead me on level ground.

Psalm 143:8–10

Likewise the Spirit also helps us in our weakness, for we do not know how to pray as we should; instead, the Spirit himself pleads for us with inexpressible groanings, and the One who is able to see what is in the heart knows what the Spirit wishes, because the Spirit intercedes for the saints in accordance with God's will.

Romans 8:26–27

Remember

He saved us through the bath of rebirth
    and renewal in the Holy Spirit . . .
so that we might be restored to
    fellowship with God by his grace
and become heirs in hope of eternal life.

Titus 3:5–7

Pray

Lord our God, may the Holy Spirit transform our hearts and increase in us the fruits of *charity, joy, peace, patience, kindness, goodness, generosity, gentleness, faithfulness, modesty, self-control,* and *chastity*. May we reach out to others, doing all we can to build up your kingdom here on earth. We ask this through your Son, our Lord Jesus Christ, in the unity of the Holy Spirit, one God forever and ever. Amen.

Glory to the Father . . . (three times)

Day Six

We Are Gifts: Each of Us for the Good of Others

Pray

Lord our God, through the light of your Holy Spirit you instruct the hearts of the faithful, your sons and daughters. Grant that we may always be docile to the Spirit working in our lives, that we may know and appreciate what is right and good and so find happiness in your presence. Help us to recognize the Spirit's invitation to service and respond with joy and eagerness. We ask this through your Son, Jesus Christ our Lord, in the unity of the Holy Spirit, one God forever and ever. Amen.

Read and Ponder

> Some manifestation of the Spirit is given to each for the common good. To one it may be given to speak wisdom through the Spirit, to another it is given to speak deep knowledge according to the same Spirit. To still another faith may be given through the same Spirit, while to another the one Spirit will give healing gifts. To one may be given the ability to perform miracles, to another the gift of prophecy, to one the gift of distinguishing spirits, to another various tongues, to still another the interpretation of tongues. One and the same Spirit causes all this, distributing individually to each as he wishes.
>
> 1 Corinthians 12:7–11

Remember

He saved us through the bath of rebirth
  and renewal in the Holy Spirit . . .
so that we might be restored to

fellowship with God by his grace
and become heirs in hope of eternal life.

Titus 3:5–7

Pray

Lord our God, may the Holy Spirit transform our hearts and increase in us the fruits of *charity, joy, peace, patience, kindness, goodness, generosity, gentleness, faithfulness, modesty, self-control,* and *chastity*. May we reach out to others, doing all we can to build up your kingdom here on earth. We ask this through your Son, our Lord Jesus Christ, in the unity of the Holy Spirit, one God forever and ever. Amen.

Glory to the Father . . . (three times)

Day Seven

Whoever Lives by the Spirit Is Free

Pray

Lord our God, through the light of your Holy Spirit you instruct the hearts of the faithful, your sons and daughters. Grant that we may always be docile to the Spirit working in our lives, that we may know and appreciate what is right and good and so find happiness in your presence. Help us to recognize the Spirit's invitation to service and respond with joy and eagerness. We ask this through your Son, Jesus Christ our Lord, in the unity of the Holy Spirit, one God forever and ever. Amen.

Read and Ponder

> We pray that you will be strengthened with all the power of his glorious might so that your steadfastness and patience will be perfected and you may joyfully give thanks to the Father who made you worthy to share in the portion of the saints in light. He has rescued us from the power of darkness and has brought us into the kingdom of his

beloved Son, by whom we are redeemed and our sins forgiven.

COLOSSIANS 1:11–14

The Spirit's fruit is love, joy, peace, patience, kindness, goodness, faith, gentleness, and self-control. There is no law against these things! Those who belong to Christ have crucified the flesh with its passions and desires. If we live in the Spirit, let us also follow the Spirit.

GALATIANS 5:18, 22–25

Remember

He saved us through the bath of rebirth
and renewal in the Holy Spirit . . .
so that we might be restored to
fellowship with God by his grace
and become heirs in hope of eternal life.

TITUS 3:5–7

Pray

Lord our God, may the Holy Spirit transform our hearts and increase in us the fruits of *charity, joy, peace, patience, kindness, goodness, generosity, gentleness, faithfulness, modesty, self-control,* and *chastity*. May we reach out to others, doing all we can to build up your kingdom here on earth. We ask this through your Son, our Lord Jesus Christ, in the unity of the Holy Spirit, one God forever and ever. Amen.

Glory to the Father . . . (three times)

Day Eight

The Spirit Guides Our Witness

Pray

Lord our God, through the light of your Holy Spirit you instruct the hearts of the faithful, your sons and daughters. Grant that we may always be docile to the Spirit working in our lives, that we may know and appreciate what is right and good and so find happiness in your presence. Help us to recognize the Spirit's invitation to service and respond with joy and eagerness. We ask this through your Son, Jesus Christ our Lord, in the unity of the Holy Spirit, one God forever and ever. Amen.

Read and Ponder

But when he comes—
the Spirit of truth—
he will lead you to the whole truth,
for he will not speak on his own,
but instead he will say what he hears,
and he will proclaim to you the things to come.

JOHN 16:13

And when they lead you
to hand you over,
do not worry ahead of time
what you will say;
but whatever is given you in that hour,
say it;
for it will not be you speaking,
but the Holy Spirit.

MARK 13:11

Remember

He saved us through the bath of rebirth
and renewal in the Holy Spirit . . .
so that we might be restored to
fellowship with God by his grace
and become heirs in hope of eternal life.

TITUS 3:5–7

Pray

Lord our God, may the Holy Spirit transform our hearts and increase in us the fruits of *charity, joy, peace, patience, kindness, goodness, generosity, gentleness, faithfulness, modesty, self-control,* and *chastity.* May we reach out to others, doing all we can to build up your kingdom here on earth. We ask this through your Son, our Lord Jesus Christ, in the unity of the Holy Spirit, one God forever and ever. Amen.

Glory to the Father . . . (three times)

Day Nine

The Spirit Is Always with Us

Pray

Lord our God, through the light of your Holy Spirit you instruct the hearts of the faithful, your sons and daughters. Grant that we may always be docile to the Spirit working in our lives, that we may know and appreciate what is right and good and so find happiness in your presence. Help us to recognize the Spirit's invitation to service and respond with joy and eagerness. We ask this through your Son, Jesus Christ our Lord, in the unity of the Holy Spirit, one God forever and ever. Amen.

Read and Ponder

> As for me, this is my covenant with them, says the Lord: my spirit that is upon you, and my words that I have put in your mouth, shall not depart out of your mouth, or out of the mouths of your children, or out of the mouths of your children's children, says the Lord, from now on and forever.
>
> ISAIAH 59:21

> The Spirit of God dwells within you. And if anyone does not have Christ's Spirit, he does not belong to Christ. But if Christ is in you, even though your body is dead because of sin, then your spirit is alive because of righteousness. And if the Spirit of God who raised Christ from the dead dwells within you, then the One who raised Christ from the dead will give life to your dead bodies through his Spirit that dwells within you.
>
> ROMANS 8:9–11

Remember

He saved us through the bath of rebirth
    and renewal in the Holy Spirit . . .
so that we might be restored to
    fellowship with God by his grace
and become heirs in hope of eternal life.

Titus 3:5–7

Pray

Lord our God, may the Holy Spirit transform our hearts and increase in us the fruits of *charity, joy, peace, patience, kindness, goodness, generosity, gentleness, faithfulness, modesty, self-control,* and *chastity.* May we reach out to others, doing all we can to build up your kingdom here on earth. We ask this through your Son, our Lord Jesus Christ, in the unity of the Holy Spirit, one God forever and ever. Amen.

Glory to the Father . . . (three times)

Various Prayers

Prayer of Consecration

Divine Holy Spirit,
eternal Love of the Father and of the Son,
I adore you, I thank you, I love you,
and I ask you pardon for all the times
I have grieved you.
Descend with many graces during
the ordination of bishops and priests,
during the consecration of men and women
religious,
during the reception of Confirmation by all the
faithful.
Be light, holiness and zeal.
Spirit of Truth, sanctify my mind, imagination
and memory;
enlighten me.
May I know Jesus Christ our Master
and understand his Gospel and the teachings of
the Church.

Increase in me the gifts of wisdom, knowledge, understanding and counsel.
Spirit of Holiness, guide me in your will,
sustain me in the observance of the commandments
in the fulfillment of the responsibilities of my life's calling.
Grant me the gifts of fortitude and holy fear of God.
Life-giving Spirit, sanctify my heart.
Nourish and increase the divine life in me.
Grant me the gift of holiness. Amen.

Blessed James Alberione

Prayer for Enlightenment

℣. Come, Holy Spirit, fill the hearts of your faithful.
℟. And kindle in them the fire of your love.
℣. Send forth your Spirit and they shall be created.
℟. And you shall renew the face of the earth.

Let us pray.

O God, you instructed the hearts of the faithful by the light of the Holy Spirit; grant us in the same Spirit to be truly wise, and ever to rejoice in his consolation. Through Christ our Lord. Amen.

To the Spirit of Pentecost

Holy Spirit, Spirit of Pentecost,
help me to clarify what is ambiguous,
to give warmth to what is indifferent,
and to enlighten what is obscure,
so that I may be for the world
a true and generous witness of Christ's love,
because no one can live without love. Amen.

Saint John Paul II

To the Spirit of Love

Come, Holy Spirit.
Come, Mighty Spirit.
Spirit of love and wisdom,
Spirit of light and power,
you help us in our weakness.
Come, fill our inmost being.

Come, Holy Spirit, come to us.
Transform us so that our hearts may be
a new creation of your love.
Guide us with your wisdom and love,
and let the radiance of your light
renew the face of the earth. Amen.

Come, Spirit, Our Creator

(Veni Creator Spiritus)

O Spirit and our Creator,
Come and dwell in every soul you have made.
Bring to birth the flame of love
in these hearts which belong to you.
You are our consoler and our certain hope.
You are the gift of God Most High.
You are the source of our life and the fire of
love,
anointing sent us from above.
You are the reflection of the Father's love,
the fulfillment of his promise, too.
You stir in us the gift of grace,
putting your wisdom upon our lips.

Your seven gifts give to your flock.
Come, fill our hearts with your own love.
You are our everlasting joy.
You are the power which can never fail.
From danger save us, Mighty One.
And help us follow Christ the Son.
Through darkness, pain and through every loss
our hope is certain, trusting in you.
Most Holy Trinity on high—
The Father, Son and Spirit one.—
your people praise you with all their heart,
longing for heaven, O vision blest!

Holy Spirit, Come

(Veni Sancte Spiritus)

Come, Holy Spirit, come
from your celestial home.
Send forth the radiance of your light.
Come, Father of the poor!
Come with gifts that endure.
Come, light of every heart.
Greatest comforter of all.

Sweetest guest of the soul.
Sweet refreshment here below.
In labor, you are comfort sweet,
pleasant coolness in the heat,
solace from our tears.
O blessed Light divine,
Visit these hearts of thine;
Fill our inmost being.
Without you, Spirit, and your grace
nothing pure in us will stay.
Any good is turned to ill.
What is soiled, make it pure.
What is wounded, work a cure.
Wash away our guilt.
Gently bend the rigid heart.
To what is frozen, your warmth impart.
Redirect our errant ways.
Fill the faithful, who confide
in your power to guard and guide,
with your sevenfold gifts.
To us, grace and mercy send.
Grant salvation at life's end.
Eternal joy, forever.
Amen. Alleluia.

For an Outpouring of the Holy Spirit

Holy Spirit, Lord and Giver of life,
you, who came down upon the Apostles
in a mighty wind and with fire,
who filled the house where they were and
gave them the gift of tongues
to proclaim the wonders of God, come down
now upon me also.
Fill me with yourself;
and make of me a temple wherein you dwell.
Open my lips to proclaim your praise,
to ask your guidance,
and to declare your love.
Holy Light, divine Fire, eternal Might,
enlighten my mind to know you,
inflame my heart to love you,
strengthen my will to seek and find you.
Be for me
the living and life-giving Breath of God,
the very air I breathe,
and the only sky in which my spirit soars.

Prayer for Holiness of Life

Breathe in me, O Holy Spirit,
that my thoughts may all be holy.
Act in me, O Holy Spirit,
that my work, too, may be holy.
Draw my heart, O Holy Spirit,
that I may love only what is holy.
Strengthen me, O Holy Spirit,
that I may defend all that is holy.
Guard me, O Holy Spirit,
that I may always be holy.

Saint Augustine

Divine Praises in Honor of the Holy Spirit

Glory to the Holy Spirit forever.
Glory to the Comforter forever.
Glory to the Spirit of truth forever.
Glory to the Spirit of grace and prayer forever.
Glory to the Spirit of Jesus forever.
Glory to the Spirit of the Father and the Son forever.

Glory to the Third Person of the adorable Trinity forever.

Blessed James Alberione

To Obtain the Gifts of the Holy Spirit

Come, Holy Spirit, Spirit of Wisdom! Teach us to discern and love the wisdom of the Lord. Your fire tests all wisdom of this world. Your wind overturns the mighty and raises up the lowly.

Come, Holy Spirit, Spirit of Understanding! You alone know the mind of God. Only in you can we fathom the mysteries of divine revelation; only through you do we recognize the path we are called to follow. Enlighten our minds.

Come, Holy Spirit, Spirit of Counsel! You banish doubt and uncertainty. Through you is the will of God revealed to us. Help and guide us in living this will.

Come, Holy Spirit, Spirit of Fortitude! Uphold us when we are weak. In your strength the apostles, martyrs, and confessors found the courage to witness to Christ with their very lives.

Come, Holy Spirit, Spirit of Knowledge! In creation we recognize your might, in revelation your wisdom, in our redemption your love. Teach us to see everything in relation to God.

Come, Holy Spirit, Spirit of Piety! Enkindle in us divine love. In you we have received the spirit of adoption as sons and daughters so that full of joy we dare to cry: *Abba, loving Father!*

To Obtain the Fruits of the Holy Spirit

Lord Jesus, by myself I can do nothing, but with the help of your grace I can do all things. And so, with all my heart and in the name of Jesus:

I reject the spirit of anger and humbly implore your Holy Spirit for the virtues of meekness and gentleness.

I reject the spirit of greed and implore your Holy Spirit for the virtue of generosity.

I reject the spirit of sloth and implore your Holy Spirit for the virtues of diligence and fidelity.

I reject the spirit of pride and implore your Holy Spirit for the virtues of humility and poverty of spirit.

I reject the spirit of lust and implore your Holy Spirit for the virtues of chastity and purity of heart.

I reject the spirit of gluttony and implore your Holy Spirit for the virtues of temperance and self-control.

I reject the spirit of envy and implore your Holy Spirit for the virtues of charity, joy, and peace.

That Christ May Live in Me

Holy Spirit, vivify me;
Love of God, consume me;
the way of Truth, lead me;
with your grace, empower me.
You are the Promised One
sent by the Father,
reminding us of all
that Jesus Master taught.
I ask you for no other knowledge,
no other wisdom
than that of Christ Crucified—
and that he may live in me!

For One's Family and Friends

Holy Spirit, Love of the Father and the Son,
hear my prayer for all those
whom you have given me to love.
By the love you have for them I pray you,
protect them from all harm,
deliver them from evil,
comfort them in sorrow,
reassure them in anxiety,
give them your own joy,
and draw them to yourself.

In Every Need

Holy Spirit,
my light, my love, my strength,
be with me now and always.
In all my doubts, anxieties and trials,
  come, Holy Spirit.
In hours of loneliness, weariness and grief,
  come, Holy Spirit.
In failure, in loss and in disappointment,
  come, Holy Spirit;

When others fail me, when I fail myself,
come, Holy Spirit.
When I am ill, unable to work, depressed,
come, Holy Spirit.
Now and forever, and in all things,
come, Holy Spirit.

For Discernment

Almighty God, we ask you to send
your Holy Spirit into our hearts
that we may be directed according to your will.
Defend us from error, and guide us to all truth
so that, steadfast in faith, we may increase in love
and in all good works.
We ask this through your Son, Jesus Christ our
Lord. Amen.

An Evangelizer's Prayer

Spirit of Wisdom, Communication of the Father and of the Son, open my heart to hear your voice as I try to discern God's will and the new ways you are opening up for evangelization.

Help me grow in discernment, critical reflection, and apostolic fruitfulness. Make me attentive to the appeals of the Church and of the world in the search for pastoral priorities and programs, in an effort to share the faith in all its beauty and richness.

May I proclaim Christ in a way that shows others the profound joy that comes from embracing life in him.

I trust in the power of your inspiration and take courage in your promise: "Proclaim the good news to all creation; I am with you always."

To the Holy Spirit of Grace

O Holy Spirit of Grace,
be my wisdom, to teach me faith;
be my understanding in doubt;
be my courage and strength against temptation;
be my right judgment in fulfilling my vocation;
be my love in all my actions;
be my holy reverence all the day long,
that you may be my comfort at the last
and my happiness forever. Amen.

For Purity of Heart

O Holy Spirit,
living water and radiant fire.
Cleanse my heart with the outpouring of your grace
and fill it with the fire of your love.
Holy Spirit, God of Love,
dwell forever in my heart.

For Those Who Are Far from God

O Holy Spirit,
may the power of your love be felt in the hearts of all men and women.
Let your light shine ever more brightly on those
who are wandering in the darkness, far from God.
Turn them to the life-giving Heart of Jesus
and to the healing powers of his precious Blood.

For the Dying

Holy Spirit, be present to all who are dying: sustain them with your power; console them with your love. Even in their sufferings, fill them with your joy. When their eyes close to the things of this world, grant that they may open them again to gaze on you, O Unfailing Light.

Grant that they may rest in the eternal possession of you.

Prayer for the Souls in Purgatory

The souls of the faithful departed are your temples, gracious Spirit; you watch over them, love them and help them in their pain. Spirit of Consolation, let them know the comfort of your care and the tenderness of your love.

Prayer to the Holy Spirit, the Secret of Sanctity

by Désiré-Joseph Cardinal Mercier

I am going to reveal to you the secret of sanctity and happiness. Every day for five minutes control your imagination and close your eyes to all the noises of the world in order to enter into yourself. Then, in the sanctuary of your baptized soul, which is the temple of the Holy Spirit, speak to that Divine Spirit, saying to him:

O Holy Spirit, beloved of my soul, I adore you.
Enlighten me, guide me,
strengthen me, console me.
Tell me what I should do—direct me.
I promise to submit myself to all that you ask of me,
and I accept all that you permit to happen to me.
Let me only know your will.

If you do this, your life will flow along happily, serenely, and full of consolation, even in the midst of trials. Grace will be proportioned to the trial, giving you the strength to carry it even until you arrive at the gate of paradise, laden with merit. This submission to the Holy Spirit is the secret of sanctity.

Invocations to the Holy Spirit

Spirit of Faith, help us overcome the difficulties and trials of life.

Spirit of Truth, give us delight in every word that comes from the mouth of God.

Spirit of Light, illumine the darkness.

Spirit of Fidelity, make us faithful witnesses of your love.

Spirit of Piety, pray in us with a longing that cannot be expressed in words.

Spirit of Life, live in us with your life of grace and love.

Spirit of Newness, reawaken in us daily a new heart and a new spirit.

Spirit of Fruitfulness, produce in us living waters, flowing out to all who thirst.

Spirit of Adoption, renew in us the awareness that we are all children of God.

Spirit of Holiness, fashion and protect in us the image of the Son, so that we may become as the Father has predestined us.

Spirit of Power, conquer through strength

and mildness every obstacle to grace, both within and without.

Spirit of Glory, draw everyone together, that we may be one with you, with the Father and the Son, united forever in the kingdom of eternal love.

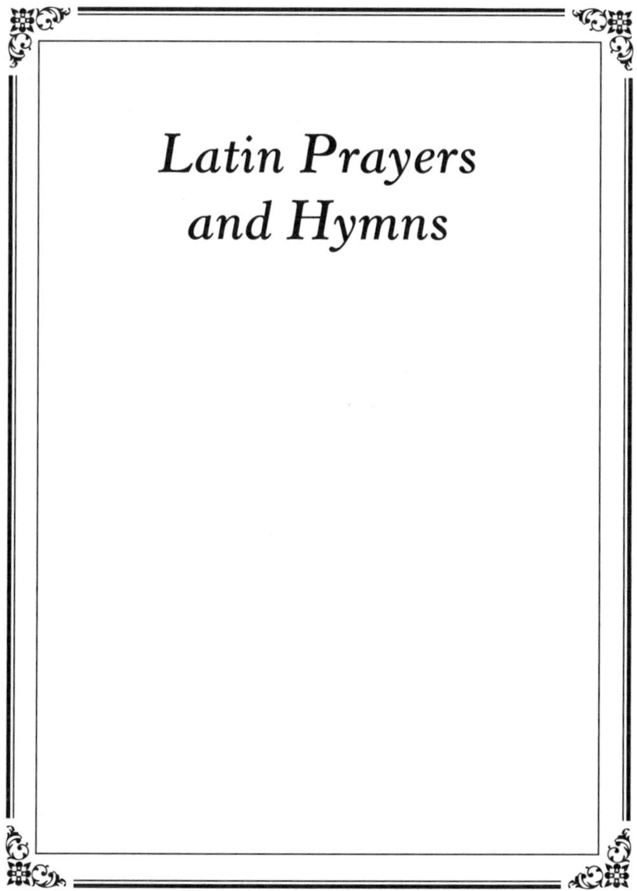

Latin Prayers and Hymns

Emitte Spiritum tuum

Veni, Sancte Spiritus, reple tuorum corda fidelium, et tui amoris in eis ignem accende

℣. Emitte Spiritum tuum et creabuntur;

℟. Et renovabis faciem terrae.

Oremus:

Deus, qui corda fidelium Sancti Spiritus illustratione docuisti: da nobis in eodem Spiritu recta sapere, et de eius semper consolatione gaudere. Per Christum Dominum nostrum. Amen.

Veni, Creator Spiritus

Veni, creator Spiritus
mentes tuorum visita,
imple superna gratia,
quae tu creasti pectora.
Qui diceris Paraclitus,
altissimi donum Dei,
fons vivus, ignis, caritas

et spiritalis unctio.
Tu septiformis munere,
digitus paternae dexterae
tu rite promissum Patris
sermone ditans guttura.
Accende lumen sensibus,
infunde amorem cordibus,
infirma nostri corporis,
virtute firmans perpeti.
Hostem repellas longius
pacemque dones protinus;
ductore sic te praevio
vitemus omne noxium.
Per te sciamus da Patrem
noscamus atque Filium,
te utriusque Spiritum
credamus omni tempore.
Deo Patri sit gloria,
et Filio qui a mortuis
Surrexit, ac Paraclito,
in saeculorum saecula.
Amen.

Veni, Sancte Spiritus

Veni, Sancte Spiritus,
et emitte caelitus
lucis tuae radium.
Veni, pater pauperum,
veni, dator munerum
veni, lumen cordium.
Consolator optime,
dulcis hospes animae,
dulce refrigerium.
In labore requies,
in aestu temperies
in fletu solatium.
O lux beatissima,
reple cordis intima
tuorum fidelium.
Sine tuo numine,
nihil est in homine,
nihil est innoxium.
Lava quod est sordidum,
riga quod est aridum,
sana quod est saucium.
Flecte quod est rigidum,

fove quod est frigidum,
rege quod est devium.
Da tuis fidelibus,
in te confidentibus,
sacrum septenarium.
Da virtutis meritum,
da salutis exitum,
da perenne gaudium.
Amen. Alleluia.

Suggested Reading

Caster, Gary. *Inspired: The Powerful Presence of the Holy Spirit*. Ann Arbor: Servant Books, 2015.

Durrwell, François-Xavier. *Holy Spirit of God: An Essay in Biblical Theology*. Ann Arbor: Servant Books, 2006.

Martinez, Luis M. (Archbishop). *The Sanctifier, The Classic Work on the Holy Spirit*. Boston: Pauline Books & Media, 2003. www.pauline.org

Montague, George T. *Holy Spirit, Make Your Home in Me: Biblical Meditations on Receiving the Gift of the Holy Spirit*. Frederick: Word Among Us Publications, 2008.

Pivonka, Dave. *Breath of God: Living a Life Led by the Holy Spirit*. Notre Dame: Ave Maria Press, 2015. www.avemariapress.com

List of Contributors

Thank You.

Your purchase of this book and engagement with our other projects supports us in the work we do as Daughters of St. Paul. This book is the fruit of our consecrated life, prayer, and mission of communicating God's love.

We hold you and all your intentions in our prayers. We invite you to connect with us or send us prayer intentions at pauline.org.